"This one's for you"

Poems for the
Bar/Bat Mitzvah
Candle Lighting Ceremony

www.Barmitzvahpoems.com

Written by
Marcy Schwarz

All material is copyrighted
And may not be reproduced without
prior authorization

"This one's for you"

ISBN 0-9742934-0-7

Ordering information or questions contact:

www.BarMitzvahPoems.com
or email: Marcyandcompany@aol.com

ACKNOWLEDGEMENTS
This book is dedicated to the three men in my life,
Harlan, Grant and Scott. You three keep me on my toes.
I love you.
Oh, and Mom, I am me because of you. Thanks.

Table of Contents

Chapter 1
How This Book Came To Be

A few years ago, when my friends were starting to host their "first rounds" of Bar/Bat Mitzvahs, I made a discovery. I found out that the thought of writing the poems needed for their children's candle lighting ceremonies made my otherwise normal, intelligent, successful friends -- nuts. They were spending thousands of dollars on their affairs; coordinating florists, caterers, music, formalwear, transportation for fifty of their child's closest friends and who knows what else, but were stumped and crazed over the poems.

Because I was an advertising person by trade and just naturally creative (I can thank my parents for that), friends asked me to write their children's poems. It was my pleasure to help my friends. After all, I knew their families almost as well as they did. So it was easy for me; it came to me like second nature.

I don't actually remember which one of my pals asked me to write the poems for a friend of hers. But one of them did. I thought it over, said, "sure" and charged the woman a fair price. She loved the poems and told some of her friends. Then, friends of friends started calling me; and so on.

My husband (also in advertising) and I thought it might be a nice side business for me. We decided to give it the old college try. And, it worked. For seven years I wrote candle lighting poems for clients I obtained through word of mouth.

It was going so well, I wanted to expand my business and reach more people. We knew the best way to reach the most people was on the new, emerging Internet. The first step was to choose a name for our website. We thought: what could be better than calling a company that writes Bar Mitzvah poems, BarMitzvahPoems.com? Luckily, no one had yet registered the name and BarMitzvahPoems.com was ours. With the help of additional staffing, we've written hundreds of candle lighting ceremonies.

Over the years, many clients have told me they wish they had some kind of book with prepared poems to refer to, sort of a *Bar Mitzvah Poems for*

Dummies. No one has written one yet, so here we are. I've taken over 250 of our best poems and written them down for you. I've tried to include every possible scenario you may encounter. Chapter 5 clearly tells you exactly how to use these poems and craft them into your own personalized ceremony.

Chapter 2
The Origins of the Candle Lighting Ceremony

Ahhh, the candle lighting ceremony - a wonderful and frightening tradition. I tried to ascertain where this time honored tradition began; but I couldn't track its' trail. When my brother, Steven, was a Bar Mitzvah in 1964, he didn't have to worry about rehearsing for a candle lighting ceremony. The bandleader (no such thing as DJ's back then) called out the names of each person invited to come up and light a candle. He played a different song for each person or group that came up and all Steven had to do is hand them the lighted candle, smile for the photographer and wipe off the kisses after the candle lighting smoocher turned his/her back.

Besides, he had enough to worry about. Learning his Haftarah and wondering which girls to invite was just about all he could handle. We all had to live through the "Grandma's dress is wrong" debacle, too. What a nightmare. But that's for another book.

The next Bar Mitzvah I attended was for Steven's son, Gregory, in 1989. I had never even heard of a candle lighting ceremony. In fact, I was in the bathroom when the ceremony began. People came rushing in yelling and searching the stalls for Aunt Marcy.

They were actually upset with me that I was not in the ballroom and waiting for my poem to be recited. I didn't even know that the whole ceremony existed until that moment. They had to stop the whole Bar Mitzvah while they searched for me. I was sorry but what could I say? Perhaps they should have told me about it before I went to the ladies room. Anyway, by the time my first son made his Bar Mitzvah in 1995, it was already a tradition for the Bar Mitzvah boy/girl to have yet another thing to worry about before the big day.

Getting back to why we have candle lighting poems, the best I could determine, is the Bar Mitzvah coincides with the child's 13th birthday (that is unless he is born in February and all your elderly relatives live in Florida and you don't want them to come north and face the bitter cold, so you change the Bar Mitzvah date to April). That is to say, upon turning 13, the child is welcomed into the Jewish community as an adult. We celebrate his/her birthday with a party. The caterer offers you a cake (not gratis) and you take it. It's very rare when they wheel out the cake and everyone just sings *Happy Birthday,* although I have seen it done. Someone, somewhere said, "As long as we are bringing up all our beloved relatives, lets make it less boring and write a cute little ditty for each." And, so, we have the birth of the candle lighting ceremony. *Of course, this is not written in stone anywhere; it's all conjecture on my part!*

All I know is that most people do it and few enjoy the process. Some parents decide to let the Bar/Bat Mitzvah child write his or her own poems. That's cool as long as they don't expect too much and don't get angry when they don't get much. It has been my experience that most twelve-year old kids don't care or don't want to take the time to write the poems. I get e-mails all the time on our website from kids that are begging me to help them write their poems. They are so used to finding everything they need for every school project on the Internet. They just type *Bar Mitzvah poems* in the search engine and up we come. I understand this since I have two kids of my own who find everything they need online. I can't remember the last time one asked me to take him to the library to do any kind of research. In fact, as it turns out, we can go online in our house and access the library's records. Amazing.

Anyway, since this is a business, I can't give them a free ride, but I do tell them to relax and just try and write what's in their heart; nothing too long or fancy. I have even started some kids off (the really needy, pathetic ones) on the road to creating their own candle lighting ceremony. I have needy, pathetic kids, too when it's time for them to do a project that takes more than 15 minutes to complete.

Chapter 3
The Candle Lighting Ceremony

You want to honor those people who mean so much to you and your family. At the same time, you must ask relatives who don't have *any kind* of relationship at all to your child. You'd probably rather not ask these people, but out of respect to your or your spouse's parents, you feel as if you must.

Well the truth is, you must. I am a firm believer in "doing the right thing." It's not worth the fight with your mother if you don't ask Great Aunt Sybil to light a candle. Truth is you don't know what to say about her. You hardly even know her. She's been living in Florida for the past 35 years and you didn't like her all that much before she moved down. Forget it. You gotta do what you gotta do. Life's too short to waste energy on this kind of stuff.

The whole event is an energy-consuming nightmare. As some wonderfully, intelligent philosopher once said, "Don't sweat the small stuff." Give her the candle and you can use it as leverage with your mother some day when you really need it. We have some written here that are perfect. Not too personal because that would be obviously phony. They are nice and generic.

The candle lighting ceremony begins after the family of the Bar/ Bat Mitzvah makes their grand entrance into the ballroom. Everybody does the hora. Then the ***Kiddush*** *(prayer over the wine)* and the ***Hamotzei*** *(prayer over the challah)* are said and the candle lighting ceremony begins.

By the way, it is rare when there are only thirteen candles. Most ceremonies include a good luck (14th) candle. In fact, most we write have at least 15 candles. Be sure to find out if your caterer supplies the candles. If he does, be sure to tell him how many candles you need on the cake. I've seen ceremonies where there were not enough candles and everyone gets so nervous. If this happens at your affair, don't panic. Just, **nonchalantly** put out (you know, have your husband lick his thumb and forefinger) the flames from the number of candles you are short. It usually runs out just about the time you are supposed to go up and light your candle anyway.

The following is the order most people follow for the candle lighting ceremony. Of course it is up to you, but this is the customary order:

Welcome
Memorial candle, if you are having one, is usually first
Grandparents
Aunt & Uncles (with their kids, unless there is a really close cousin relationship and your child wants them to have their own candles)
Older relatives
Younger relatives
Friends of parents
Friends of Bar/Bat Mitzvah
Siblings
Parents
Good luck candle

The memorial candle is customarily the first candle. This is a time you can acknowledge the loss of a beloved relative. Try to add something personal to the poem, if you can. It means so much to the close relatives of the deceased person that the child remembers something specific. See the memorial candle pages for some ideas.

There are three ways to end the candle lighting ceremony: The parents light the last one after a poem is read by the Bar Mitzvah, the Bar Mitzvah recites a "good luck" candle or the parents recite the last one, using it as an opportunity to add a few closing words of love and thanks to their child and guests. Any one of these choices is fine. In fact, you can have the parents' candle as the 12th and the good luck candle as the 13th.

Since the parents are always the last to be invited up, you are there anyway. You can just stand next to your child and wait to help blow out the candles after he says the good luck poem. Or, if you prefer, you can all blow out the candles together after the parents' poem. Keep the siblings close at hand; the photographer likes to take a picture of the whole family blowing out the candles. We have included some nice poems for parents to say to their children.

Chapter 4
Stress
Don't Let It Get You

Now let's go on to the part I find most important...your stress level. If you are reading this book, it's safe to assume A) your child doesn't want to write his own poems B) you don't have the *kayach (*Yiddish for *strength)* to put aside the hours it's going to take to be creative (besides, it took all your *gidult;* also Yiddish for *strength,* to make the list of who will or will not be asked to light a candle. Deciding what songs the DJ will play for them while they walk up took another few days. Let's not even think about the dreaded seating arrangements.) C) you think you don't have a creative bone in your body or D) you assumed your child was writing her poems while she assumed you would pick up the slack at the last moment and now it's getting really, really close to the date. Whatever the reason, here you are and we are going to help you through.

What I am about to say may shock or upset you, but the truth is you shouldn't spend too much time worrying about the candle lighting poems. Yes, the ceremony is beautiful. All eyes are on the people you and your child love most. You want everyone to love his/her poems. You want the memorial candle to be meaningful and heartfelt. You want it personal and perfect.   I don't blame you. But, the truth is, this is what goes on during the candle lighting ceremony:

- Friends, who don't know your relatives well, will start to put the names together with the faces. They will start to gossip with their friends at their table about your relatives. They will recall the stories you told them about your cousin on your Mom's side. (Remember, you told them those stories, so you can't help if they gossip and snicker.)
- Your friend's dress is fantastic and everyone is commenting on her style.
- Someone dyed the gray out of his hair and it is now the topic of controversy; does it look good or ridiculous?

The point is that after about the sixth or seventh candle, most people are not listening anymore. They have lost interest. They have stopped applauding for each relative as they walk up. The roar of applause that

Bubby got for the second candle is gone now while Cousin Ira is lighting candle eight. You are losing your audience. Even if they are listening, it's rare when they can hear the poems from across the room anyway.

If you really care if anyone is listening, before the big day ask a good friend (preferably one with a big mouth and outgoing personality) to start to clap and hoot after a name is called if she senses the crowd is losing interest. This action will start his/her table to join in and hopefully, others will follow suit. Many times, there is nothing you can do until the siblings start to come up. The audience is very receptive to the adorable little sister or brother or the beautiful/handsome older siblings (many of whom they haven't seen since the last family Bar Mitzvah). Their poems are usually cute and funny, too, so the guests tend to listen to these.

Then it's your turn. Everyone gets excited for the Parents' Candle. It's the least they can do. They want to honor their host and hostess so they stop chatting and listen to this one. Many times, they give the parents a standing ovation. It's nice when they do.

These are but a few of the reasons I implore you not to make yourself crazy. No one will notice enough to warrant the stress. I can't repeat myself enough; you have so many other things to stress over before the big day, try not to worry about this, too.

Also, I recommend you try to keep the ceremony as short a possible. Try to group relatives together. See if you can bring Great Aunt Susie *and* her children, older cousins Bev and Harry, up at the same time. Write one verse for each couple/person and it will make your ceremony shorter and more tolerable for your guests.

Other ways to shorten the ceremony:
- Don't separate school and home friends from camp friends, do one friends' candle. It is fine if your child has one or two best friends to give them their own candle.
- Do not try to rhyme the names of the kids in your child's friends' candle. Just use, "all my friends" when you invite them up.
- Unless one family of your adult friends is very special to you, group more than one family together. You can bring up five six couples at the same time. Just use their names in the poem. It's fun; everyone laughs at these huge groups.

- Don't give every single out-of–town guest a candle.
- Don't make each poem 10 lines long.
- Don't give everyone you ever met in your life, his or her own candle.

Make sure your DJ has a copy of the poems. He is the one that repeats the names of each person expected to come up. It will be noisy as your child says each poem and if you've kept it a surprise, those you are calling up (sitting on the other side of the room) will not even realize that they were called up to the cake. The DJ will repeat the name(s) and the dancers (if you have them) will dance the people up to the cake.

Having the dancers boogie your guests up is also something you should consider before the event. Do you think Grandma Ethel wants to, or has the ability to, dance her way up? If not, advise the DJ to just have the dancers walk the guests up to the cake.

If after reading this book, you still don't feel "up to" writing the poems, feel free to contact us at BarMitzvahPoems.com. We will be happy to write them for you. Keep in mind there is an extra fee added for "rush" jobs!

Oh, we can also write that Bimah speech you are so worried about. You know the one **everyone listens to!**

Chapter 5
How To Use These Poems

Go to the category you need. Read them over. Some will be perfect for you as is; some will need slight changes.

A verse is two lines. Notice that every two lines end in rhyme. It doesn't matter how many two-line verses you use for each poem. For most candle lighting guests, three verses are enough room to say what you need to without making the ceremony too long. It's OK to add a little more for the memorial, grandparent or parents' candles. As long as every two lines rhyme, you're fine.

Punctuation marks, like commas and semicolons, are used more to indicate pauses than proper punctuation.

The first couple of lines is an introduction and should be a little personal. The last verse is used to invite the guest(s) up to the cake. You can mix and match any verses that work for you. I've crafted a sample in each category showing you how to combine the various verses and turn them into the perfect poem for your needs.

Feel free to replace titles like Bubby for Grandma. We typed all words that are interchangeable in **bold face**. Some single poems can be used for couples or vice a versa. A poem that is for a family friend may be perfect for an uncle. You can change many poems from Bar Mitzvah to B'nei Mitzvah; just don't use ones that end in me because the previous line rhymes with it.

Do not try to use the candle number in each poem. It gets boring after the 4th or 5th poem and I defy you to rhyme candle thirteen with anything reasonable. But, if you feel you must use the candle numbers in the poem, use them in the sentence, not at the end. Ex: Come light *candle number six*. It's easier to use *candle number six* is for you. (See the poems for ways to integrate the candle number into the verse.)

Chapter 6
Things To Remember

1. Try not to forget anyone you simply must have lighting a candle.

2. Do not offend anyone. If you were asked to light a candle at someone's Bar/Bat Mitzvah, I don't care who he or she is; you must reciprocate. Fit them in. Even if you have to put them in a group of other people, fit them in!

3. Make a copy of the poems for the DJ, so he always knows what's going on and doesn't lose track (I've seen that happen more than once).

4. There will be no literary awards given for these poems, so don't worry if they are not perfect. If you want to add some personal info, don't worry if there are too many syllables in the line; it will be just fine.

5. Make sure the caterer supplies (or not) the candles and tell him/her how many you will need.

6. Don't Stress Out! Focus on things I can't help you with like making sure your shoes match your dress.

7. If you need help with your "Parent Speech" on the bimah…we do that too at www.BarMitzvahPoems.com.

Mazel Tov on your upcoming simcha. We wish you and your family all good things. Remember, the poems should be the least of your worries.

Chapter 7
Ceremony Worksheets

Now it's time to sit down and actually begin organizing your ceremony. I've prepared four worksheets to make it easier for you. They include: #1-All Guests To Be Honored, #2-Candles I Already Know, #3-Who Still Remains To Be Honored and #4-Candle Lighting Ceremony Guest List. Look them over first, see the samples and how they were completed.

- Start by making a list of all the people you want/must honor on worksheet #1- **All Guests To Be Honored**. Group them by families when possible.

- Fill in worksheet #2 - **Candles I Already Know** – don't worry about who gets assigned to what number candle, yet. You can make all your adjustments later after you've decided who goes up and in which groups.

    SAMPLE:
    Candle # 1 - Memorial for Poppy
    Candle # 2 - Bubby
    Candle # 3 - Grandma and Grandpa
    Candle # 4 - Aunt Rae, Uncle Alex, Ian and Dell
    Candle # 5 - Aunt Sarah, Uncle Mike, Tyler and Aaron
    Candle # 6 - Great Aunt Nin and Great Uncle Paul
    Candle # 11 - Scott's Friends
    Candle # 12 - Matthew (Brother)
    Candle # 13 - Mom and Dad
    Candle # 14 - Good Luck

On worksheet #1, cross off all the people you have just assigned to a candle. Any names remaining on worksheet #1 should be moved onto worksheet #3 – **Who Remains To Be Honored?** (Photocopy this one a few times; you're going to have a lot of cross-outs, mistakes and changes.)

How many candles do you have remaining?

In the sample, we have 4 candles left and you've got a lot more than 4 people/families listed on worksheet #3 – What to Do?

- Find a common denominator among those left and divide them up in to sub-groups…Are they all friends of your family? Are they all same family members - Great Aunts and Uncles, their children and their children? Do you have friends that vacation together? All friends from Temple? All friends you've made the first day your child went to nursery school? All great friends of your parents?

You see what I mean. Try and put as many people together as possible. It's OK to put your friends and your husband's friends together – just start with a line like, "These folks are all friends of my parents..."

Draw lines (preferably with different colored pencils) matching groups -- you know like when you were in school and you had the *matching section* of the multiple choice test. Use the same color to match as many people/families as you can. (See sample on next page.) Remember to review Chapter 4 again to see ways of shortening the ceremony.

After you have grouped all the people/families on the worksheet…see who's left. Sometimes you really do have people who do not fit into any other group. If you are absolutely, positively sure that you can't fit them with any other group…*they get their own candle*. That's all there is to it.

Don't make yourself crazy! Sometimes, you have to bite the bullet and add more candles. That's OK; just try to keep them short so you don't add to much length to the ceremony.

What if I don't have enough people? This is much easier to work with….
- Have a "welcome" and a "good luck" candle
- Give your brother and sister-in-law (child's aunt and uncle) their own candle and give their children (child's cousins) their own as well.
- Add a "parent to child" candle.
- Make a "boy" friends' candle and a separate "girl" friends' candle
- Give each "family friend" family their own candle.
- Honor out-of-town guests with a special candle.

Look through the various sections and start picking poems that are perfect for your guests.   Remember to read all the verses before you make selections. A poem in the Grandparent section might be perfect for a Great Aunt and Uncle, etc.

When you are all done, transfer the list on to worksheet #4 - **Candle Lighting Ceremony Guest List.** Notice, next to each candle, I left a blank space for you to fill in the music selection for this candle. Make a photocopy of this list and give it to your DJ; it will make life a whole lot easier for you both.

SAMPLE: WORKSHEET #3

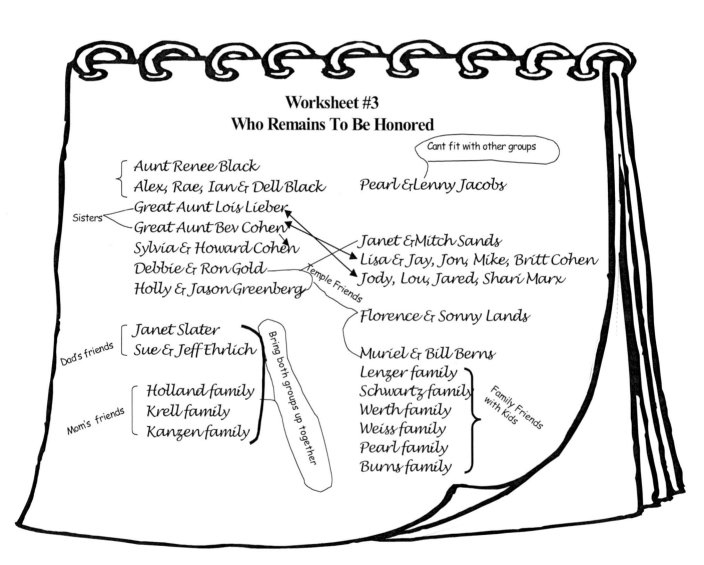

Worksheet #3
Who Remains To Be Honored

Cant fit with other groups

Aunt Renee Black
Alex, Rae, Ian & Dell Black
Pearl & Lenny Jacobs

Sisters — Great Aunt Lois Lieber
Great Aunt Bev Cohen
Sylvia & Howard Cohen   Janet & Mitch Sands
Debbie & Ron Gold   Lisa & Jay, Jon, Mike, Britt Cohen
Holly & Jason Greenberg   Jody, Lou, Jared, Shari Marx
Temple Friends

Florence & Sonny Lands

Dad's friends — Janet Slater   Muriel & Bill Berns
Sue & Jeff Ehrlich   Lenzer family
Bring both groups up together   Schwartz family
Werth family
Mom's friends — Holland family   Weiss family
Krell family   Pearl family
Kanzen family   Burns family
Family Friends with Kids

18

Worksheet #1
All Guests To Be Honored

_____

_____

_____

_____

_____

_____

_____

_____

_____

_____

_____

_____

_____

_____

_____

_____

_____

_____

_____

_____

_____

From "This One's For You" BarMitzvahPoems.com

Worksheet #2
Candles I Already Know

Candle #1 _____

Candle #2 _____

Candle #3 _____

Candle #4 _____

Candle #5 _____

Candle #6 _____

Candle #7 _____

Candle #8 _____

Candle #9 _____

Candle #10 _____

Candle #11 _____

Candle #12 _____

Candle #13 _____

Candle #14 _____

Candle #15 _____

NOTES:

Worksheet #3
Who Remains To Be Honored

_____   _____

_____   _____

_____   _____

_____   _____

_____   _____

_____   _____

_____   _____

_____   _____

_____   _____

_____   _____

_____   _____

_____   _____

_____   _____

_____   _____

_____   _____

_____   _____

NOTES:

Candle Lighting Ceremony
Guest List

Guest(s)		**Music**
Candle #1	_____	_____
Candle #2	_____	_____
Candle #3	_____	_____
Candle #4	_____	_____
Candle #5	_____	_____
Candle #6	_____	_____
Candle #7	_____	_____
Candle #8	_____	_____
Candle #9	_____	_____
Candle #10	_____	_____
Candle #11	_____	_____
Candle #12	_____	_____
Candle #13	_____	_____
Candle #14	_____	_____
Candle#	_____	_____
Candle#	_____	_____
Candle#	_____	_____
Candle#	_____	_____

Welcome Candle

If you are going to have a memorial candle, skip this one.
Otherwise, it's a nice opening.

My family and I are excited; we hope you feel that way too
I've prepared for so long, and now I am thrilled to be sharing this day
with you
I would love to honor you all here tonight, but think of the
time it would take
If I called everyone whom I love and respect; well, there just isn't room
on the cake
So let's start this candle lighting; I hope you enjoy each rhyme
Sit back, relax, clap for each one, and we'll all have a really fun time

This first candle I've dedicated, and I'll light it myself, if I may
It's for everyone who's here right now to share this wonderful day

You all make me feel so special; some have traveled so far to be
An important part of my **simcha;** thanks so much from my family and me
(special day)

I wanted to say, "Welcome and thank you," to our dear friends and family
It means so much that you came so far to be here today with me

My family and I are excited; we hope you feel that way too
I've prepared for so long and now I am thrilled to share this moment with
you

I would like to light this first candle; to say welcome and thank you, too
My family and I are especially proud to be sharing this day with you

For those who are not here with us now, I'd like to take a moment to say,
You're in our hearts, our thoughts, our minds, especially on this joyous day

So let's start this candle lighting; I hope you enjoy each rhyme
Sit back, relax, clap for each one, and well all have a really fun time

I wanted to say, "Hi and thank you". I'm so happy you all could come
So for everyone here, my family and friends, I will gladly light candle one

Memorial Candle

This is customarily the first candle. Try to add some personal information like "Grandpa taught me" or "we used to…" It's OK to make your guests a little teary.

This first candle I've dedicated to my grandparents, so lovingly
I love to hear stories about them; it makes them seem closer to me
As I took my place on the bimah, I'm sure they would have been proud
I know they would have been dancing with joy, along with this
wonderful crowd
Now as I light this candle, and its' flame is burning bright
Their memories will live on through us; their spirits are with us tonight

If you don't mind, I'll light this first candle, for my **Grandpa** who's not here today
There isn't a day I don't think of him; no words could ever convey

I know that my **Grandpa** loved me; we had great times together for sure
I wouldn't have traded a moment we've shared; I just wish we could have shared more

This first candle I've dedicated, to two people, so lovingly
My **Grandfathers Julius and Frank;** I wish they were here with me

This first candle I've dedicated, to **two** people so lovingly
Aunt Betty who lives on through the stories **Dad** tells, and **Nanny**, **her** love surrounds me

My **Aunt Roberta** is not here with us, but I'll take this moment to say
I'll always remember **her** loving ways and I feel **her** with me today

This first candle I've dedicated to my **grandfather**, so lovingly
I love to hear stories about **him;** it makes **him** seem closer to me

So this one's for you, **Zadie Stanley,** and although you are not with us here
I know your heart would have been filled with joy; cause **Zadie**, I feel you so near

I light this first candle for **Grandma,** whom I wish could have been here
I miss her smile and gentle ways; in my heart she'll always be dear

I know my **Grandma** is with me, and although **she** is not in our sight
I feel **her** love fill up this room; her spirit is with us tonight

I know my **Nana** is with me. That knowledge makes me feel OK
I feel **her** love throughout the room; **her** spirit is with us today

I really miss my **Poppy;** he taught me checkers and chess
I wish **he** were here with us tonight; to share in my success

Let's all stop and think of my **Poppy,** today as we laugh, dance and pray
I know he would have been bursting with pride. As I'm sure now he's looking my way

I'd like to light this first candle, to say welcome and thank you, too
My family and I are especially proud to be sharing this day with you

If I may, I'll take a few moments; there are some thoughts I'd like to convey
Let's pause and think of our loved ones who are sorely missed today
(my grandparents)

As I took my place on the bimah, I'm sure **he** would have been proud **(they)**
I know **he** would have been dancing with joy, along with this wonderful crowd **(they)**

Now as I light this candle and its' flame is burning bright
His memory will live on through us; **his** spirit is with us tonight

So in honor of all these people, I am very proud
To light this in their memory, before this wonderful crowd

Aunt Marsha, **so strong and good-natured**; missed so much by the family
I light this candle just for you; your memories will live on through me

Grandparents

Bubbe, I can always talk to you; I love that we can be
So honest with each other; it means the world to me
I know I can always tell you, about what's on my mind
You listen to me, you never judge; you're so thoughtful and so kind
You know what they say Bubbe; a heart feels a heart; it's true
I love you Bubbe very much, this candle is just for you
                               (candle one, etc.)

Poppy and I have so much fun; he loves to play golf with me
Grandma loves to cook and read and be surrounded by her family

Grandma and Papa, such a part of our lives; you're devoted to us completely
Your goal in life is to spoil us kids, but that's OK with me

Grandma, remember you always said, you hope to make it to my **Bar** Mitzvah day?
Well, this is it and here you are; I wouldn't have it any other way

Grandpa taught me to play poker; I'm pretty good; I can bluff my way through
And your **Seders** are so special to me; I love my place, right next to you
     (Sunday dinners, holiday dinners, etc.)

You all must meet **Grandma Carol**; she has a never-ending tan
She is so great, I'm proud to say, I am her biggest fan

My grandparents live in **Florida**. They're so busy; haven't you heard
It's hard to find them; they're running around, or they're out eating "early bird"

Nana, I can talk to you; you know just what I mean
I rely upon your great advice and you let me blow off steam

Whatever we say is between us; I know that you're true blue
I'm fortunate to have you in my life. **Grandma,** I love you

I love my **Bubbe** very much; she's kind and generous, too
Who makes the best **cookies** in town? Oh, **Bubbe**, you know it's you

Grandma is my card-playing pal; we play war and gin rummy
She's active and has so much to do, but she always has time for me

I love the stories my **Grandma** tells about our family in the "old days"
Some are funny, some are cute, some are sad and some just amaze

Grandma and Papa love me so much; it shows in all that they do
I know that I'm a lucky girl to have grandparents I love, like you

I love when I come to visit; our times together are always a source
Of laughter and love with **Nanny** and fun with **Poppy** on the golf course

Nanny and Poppy are an active pair; always running; they never relax
They're either seeing a show or eating out; those two are always making tracks

My grandparents and I have a special bond. We see each other all of the time
They are always there for my special events; **dinners at your house** are
favorites of mine   **(any activity)**

You know I always look forward, to the times together with you
I love that you **play board games** with me, and it's **fun to cook with you**, too

I don't get to see **Grandma Jean**, as much as I would like to
But you know I think you're the greatest; **Grandma Jean**; I love you

I love when we get to visit, especially when we're alone
You know you spoil me rotten and you can't do that by phone!

My grandparents and I have a special bond. We hang out and chat all the time
I love when we're together; those times are favorites of mine

I have so many memories of the times and love shared with you
Not every kid is so lucky, but I know that I am; it's true

My **Grandmother** lives in **Florida**. Her hair is, you know, "Jewish red"
Whenever we are together, she makes sure that I'm very well fed

My **Grandma** enjoys playing bingo and shopping the flea markets, too
You're so much fun to be with; **Grandma**, I love you

Grandma, I'm filled with the memories of the times and the love shared with you
You never say no. You spend time with me. I'm a lucky **girl**; it's true

Grandma's so great at entertaining; your **holidays** get an awesome review
(dinners, meals, etc.)
You're food is so good, you're home so inviting; Martha Stewart could learn plenty from you

My Poppy can build anything; just ask and his talents shine through
And best of all, he goes out of his way, to make it perfect for you

I love to watch the two of you dance; Fred and Ginger have nothing on you
I love you **Grandma and Grandpa;** I'm so lucky to have both of you

And though we speak each day by phone, I love when **Nana** stays
We take our walks and share our thoughts, growing closer every day

I love you **Grandma and Grandpa;** you two have always been there for me
I know you love me as I love you; I feel blessed that we're family

When I think of my **Bubby**, so many words come into mind
Cheerful, beautiful, positive, generous, loving and so kind

My **Grandma** lives in sunny Florida; I don't get to see her that much
I miss her not living near me, but we always keep in touch

Grandma loves music and art. She hangs with friends and loves to read
She plays golf and goes to theater; she is very active indeed

You always come to visit us; wherever we may live
I always look forward to those times and all the love you give

You two are so full of life; you sure don't look your age **(Nana, you're)**
I bet when you were younger, you **guys** were "all the rage"

You know I always look forward, to my visits with you two
You are so much fun to be with; I have wonderful times with you

This candle is for my Grandparents; there are some things I'd like to say
I'm honored the two of you are here; to share my joy today

I know you don't think we call you enough; that's no reflection on you
As kids we're so busy; our activities don't stop, and we have so much to do

Great Grandma Flossie is so much fun; she's kind and loving and sweet
I think that she is very smart; the wisest lady you'll ever meet

My Grandparents are "Snowbirds"; most of the time they don't live here
I don't get to see them as much as I'd like, but in my heart, they are always near

*****

But most of all what I really love is just being together, it's true
Grandma, please come be with me now; this candle is just for you

My grandparents make me feel special; all they do shows their unique touch
Please come light this candle now. **Grandma and Poppy**, I love you so much

And now if you'll honor me **Bubbe,** this candle is just for you
I'll never forget what you mean in my life. Come up **Bubbe**, I love you

Please come up now **Grandma** and light candle number two
You know how important you are in my life; **Grandma**, I love you

Please come up **Nanny and Poppy;** this candle is just for you two
You know how much you mean to me; I love you both, I do

Now come up **Nanny and Poppy;** I want you to stand here with me
I'm so lucky to have you both in my life. Please come up and light candle three

Please come up **Nanny and Poppy;** this candle is just for you two
I really do wish you lived closer; **Nanny and Poppy**, I love you

Grandma and Grandpa, it's your turn to come up and stand here with me
I love you both, and you know that, you mean so much to our family

My grandparents are a great part of my life; I am lucky to have you two
Please honor me now by coming up. **Grandma and Grandpa,** I love you
Or
I love you both, now please come up and light candle two

Grandma makes me feel special; when we visit she makes a great meal
Please come up and be with me **Grandma;** I love you; you know how I feel

We don't get to see you as much as we'd like; miles between our homes
don't allow
But we love you and think of you often, please come up and be with me now
(This one can be used in any category)

I love you **Grandma and Poppy;** I'll always cherish my time with you
Please honor me now by coming up and lighting candle number two

I love you **Nana and Poppy;** you mean so much me
Please honor me now by coming up and lighting candle number three

Grandma Gertie, I love you; you are so important to me
Please honor me now, by coming up, and lighting candle number three

Nana, now it's your turn to come and stand with me here
I love you and wish you lived closer; you know in my heart you're so dear
(I'm so lucky you are my Nana)

Aunts & Uncles

Check in the family friends' category, you may find ones that are suitable for aunts and uncles.

When Mom says no to our wishes and whims, there's one person we always run to
We can count on Aunt Joan to be on my side. What would we do without you?
We've always been so very close; on you we can depend
You are more than just our aunt; you are our special friend
Please come and be with us now; we've saved this candle for you
We're so happy to have each other; Aunt Joan, we love you

Uncle Mike, you know you've inspired me; I want to be a **doctor** just like you
You work so hard, your success so great; you take such pride in what you do

I love my Aunt and Uncle, and my cousins are just great
When I know you're coming here, I can hardly wait

I love when you come over; and we all sleep in my room
Don't you agree, we have such fun; the time just seems to zoom?

Another great Aunt and Uncle, live **out Staten Island** way
I'm so happy you two could be here; on this my special day

Aunt Wendy, I love your company; nothing we talk about is taboo
We go to **concerts and movies, or just hang out**; no one has an **aunt** like you   **(any activities)**

Aunt Sarah and Uncle Danny I'm so happy you've come here to be
An important part of my special day; it means so much to me

You know I love you **Uncle Geoff;** and **Claudia**, I just can't wait
Till you're married and part of our family; and we can all celebrate

Aunt Angie I love to talk to you; about "girl stuff" you are so cool
Uncle Mickey, you make me laugh all the time. You know I think you guys rule.

When Mom says no to my wishes and whims, there's one person I always run to
I can count on **Aunt Joan** to be on my side. What would I do without you?

We've always been so very close; on you I can depend
You are more than just my **aunt**; you are my special friend

I love going places with you; I'm so glad you ask me along
I love how you go out of your way, to make me feel like I really belong

I always look forward to the High Holidays; when I know I'll be with you two
Our time spent together in temple, brings me closer to both of you

With you I always have a great time; you are so awesome and cool
Uncle Jerry, I love being with you; as **uncles** go, you rule!

Aunt Bonnie is such fun to be with; we shop until we drop
Then we hide our purchases so **Uncle Marty** doesn't make us stop

Uncle Marty, you are so much fun; you're an uncle that's deluxe
We love when **Aunt Bonnie's** not looking, and slip us a couple of bucks

The parties at **Aunt Meryl's** house are always awesome indeed
She cooks and prepares so much, like she's got an army to feed

No one cooks as good as **Aunt Meryl**; you take pride in all that you do
If Martha Stewart came to **Seder** this year, she'd learn a trick or two
                    (any holiday)

Uncle Jay is the fashion **King.** He's so trendy, so stylin', so cool
I hope you know I love you; as **uncles** go, you rule

My great **Aunt Ruth** is a very sweet lady; so easy to talk to, it's true
I agree with all of the family; **Aunt Ruth** we all love you

Aunt Renee is a woman who's special. Always smiling and happy to be
Together and having a good time; I'm so glad that you're my family

I love you **Uncle Jeffery**; you show me such a great time
We laugh and play and fool around; I'm so happy that you're mine

Aunt Suzy and **Uncle Harry**; in our hearts you are so dear
It is truly an honor for me and my folks that both of you are here

*****

I wish you guys lived closer, so we could be together more
Aunt Jamie, Uncle Dave, Jon and Sammie; you know I love you four

You always give me presents; I love all the cute gifts you buy
Come on up and be with me now. **Uncle Steven**, you know you're my guy

So please come light this next candle; **for you I've saved number four
(times with you are never a bore)**
You are the most awesome **uncle**. A **nephew** couldn't ask for more

My **Aunt Barbara** is a terrific cook; **Uncle Jay** is such fun when he jokes
I love to hang with **Alex and Josh (use up to three names).** Come up now;
I love you folks

Uncle Steve and Aunt Meryl, Gregory and Craig, you, too
I'm so happy you are here with me; I've saved this candle for you

Aunt Rose and **Uncle Stanley;** I'd like you to stand here with me
I've saved this candle just for you. **So, please light candle three
(you mean so much to our family)**

Please come up **Aunt Gayle, Uncle Tom and Scott**, too
It gives me so much pleasure to share this day with you

When you're around we always laugh; you are a lot of fun
Aunt Marla, I love you, please come up and light this one

You are two wonderful people; you mean so much to our family
I love you **Aunt Karen, Uncle Jason;** please come up and be with me

Aunt Adrienne and Uncle Bobby; I'm so glad we're family
This next candle is for you both; please come up and be with me

Uncle Michael, you know I think you're cool; in you I can always confide
You're more than my **uncle**; you are my friend. Please come up and stand
by my side

It's your turn now, so please come up and light this candle with me
**Aunt Randy, Uncle Neal, Lauren and Annie (use with any name ending
with the long E sound)**

Generic Family

The poems in this section can be used for all other relatives. They are great for family members that are not too close with your child. You can make them more personal by adding information that has special meaning to your guests.

I love that I'm surrounded by my family tonight
And having you two with us, just adds to my delight
I know we don't see you too often; but some memories stand out in my mind
Like the time we went to Sea World; we had such a wonderful time
Cousin Annie and Cousin Paul, please come up right away
I'm so happy you are here with me, to share my special day

Mom talks about wonderful memories, of growing up with all of you
I love when she tells the stories. It makes me feel part of it, too

Now I'll call up my cousins, we love to hang out and play games
I think you all are so special, and I know you feel the same

We can always talk about anything; you guys really know I love you
We'll always be there for each other; and you all know that's true

I'm delighted you could come; **Bernice and Jack and crew**
I've know you guys all my life; you know how I feel about you

We don't see each other too often, because we live so far away
But **Grandma** mentions you all the time; and I'm so glad you're with us today

I love to spend Christmas with you; it's always fun to be
A part of a fun family holiday and I'm dazzled by your tree

I always look forward to Christmas; I know good times are in store
We have so much fun; it's dizzying, and I get great gifts galore

I'm honored you are coming up now, to be a part of this ritual
It means of much to my family and me; I love you and I always will

I always look forward to **Christmas**, 'cause I know I'll be with you
I love my time with the family and all the yummy food, too

You are so full of life; you sure don't look your age
I bet when you were younger, you were "all the rage"

When **Cousin Renee** is in town for a holiday; I know that she will be
Joining us to share good times and bring something special for me

Auntie Martha, even though I don't know you that well, my Mom speaks
so fondly of you
You traveled so far to be here with us; that makes me feel so special, too

We love to go to your house; where the holidays are great
When our family gets together, the good times are first rate

I love that I'm surrounded by so much family tonight
And having you **four** with us, just adds to my delight

I always look forward to the High Holidays; when I know I'll be with you
two
Our time spent together in temple, brings me closer to both of you

Susan, Dan, Geri, Robert; Beth and Gary, too
I'm so happy you are here with me; I've saved this candle for you

I love the holidays at **Jackie** and **Daniel's;** you serve enough food for an
army or two
Jackie you are an awesome cook; Martha Stewart's got nothing on you

You **four** are often on my mind; I wish that we all lived near
I'm so happy you are with me today; in my heart you're all so dear

Sandy and Bob, I hope you know, you are two of my favorite kin
I always love coming to you house especially when the whole family is in

We love our wonderful cousins, but there's some info I'm trying to glean
For the life of me, I can't figure out just what does "once removed" mean?

I love spending the holidays with you; where family and food are first rate
We sit and talk and laugh and joke; we feel stuffed from all we ate

This next candle is for you **five;** I'm excited you all could be
Such an important part of my special day; please come and stand with me

I love to go to your house. For great holidays you are the source
When you're not cooking up a super meal, we can find you on the golf
course

The next group is cousins of mine, and my feelings are very sincere
It means so much to my family and me that all of you could be here

I'd like you to meet some more of our clan; this group is terrific, you'll see
Cindy, Kenny, Karen and Bill, are second cousins to me

I love to see my **cousin Adam**; he's one of my favorite folks
He makes me laugh out loud a lot; he really tells great jokes

I know we don't see you too often; but some memories stand out in my mind
Like the time we went to **Sea World (name any place);** we had such a
wonderful time

We look forward to seeing each other; cause our family is really first rate
Our famous "cousins' get-togethers are parties that sure are great

I know I'll get a postcard, when you travel, explore and probe
Exotic spots throughout the world, as **you (two)** journey around the globe

We always have a great time; I love playing in the pool and the sun
At your house the bar-b-cues are great; we're sure to have a day filled with
fun

Dad said that he was a lucky kid to have a family like you
You know he means it from his heart; I feel the same way, too

I have more wonderful family here, that I'd like to honor tonight
So let's make room, cause with this group, things are going to get tight

We miss the holidays with you all; it's a shame you live so far away
But I'm happy you're here to be with me, to be a part of my special day

From all around **New York State**, we have our family
And I'm so glad you all could come, to share this day with me

She's the matriarch of my **father's** clan; and so important to us all
I love to hear the stories she tells, about my **dad** when he was small

Aunt Sylvia, I love you very much; I look forward to being with you
At family functions and holidays; we have such a great time; it's true

Now I'll call up my cousins, we can laugh and all discuss
How all our holiday dinners, get crazy 'cause of us

I always look forward to the **holidays (or name a specific holiday);** when I
know that we'll be together
The food is great, we have such fun; I hope it stays this way forever

I have a really cool family; my cousins are A number 1
I look forward to family functions, cause I know that we'll have so much fun

To be surrounded by my family makes today a really big treat
And having you **four** with me, helps make this day complete

Cousin Millie and Cousin Mickey; I'm so happy you've come here to be
An important part of my **simcha**; it means so much to my parents and me
                         (special day)

And cousins **Lane and Angela, Derek and Jenna**, too
I love you all and am thrilled to be, sharing this day with you

They came all the way from **Florida**, where they're **crusin'** a lot of the time
                                   (golfing or any activity)
I love when we get together; did I mention they're favorites of mine?

*****

So please come up **Susan and Stan; Joey, David and Robbie**, too
It's so nice to have my family here; especially the **five** of you

Steven, Meryl, Greg and Craig; please come up and stand here with me
I love you guys, but you know that; I'm so glad we're all family

Cousin Annie and Cousin Paul, please come up right away
I'm so happy you are here with me, to share my special day

I know we don't see you too often, but I'm so happy when we do
Please come up and be with me now, I've saved this candle for you

Susan, Billie, David and Jane, please come up without delay
I'm so happy you are here with me, the share my special day

Please come up to me right now and light a candle, too
It's so nice to have my family here, especially the **six** of you

I love hanging with you guys; we eat, and laugh and have fun
Squeeze in close as I call you; this will be a tight one

Jenny and David; I'm so glad we're family
This next candle is for you **both**; please come up and be with me

I love when we get together; we have fun whatever we do
So come on up and stand with me now; this candle is for all of you

You two always make me feel special; that's how I feel about you, too
Mandy and Stuart please come up now, this candle is meant for you

All kidding aside, I love you guys; I'm so glad we're family
Please come to light a candle, and stand here next to me

Today, I'm happy you're not on the tee; candle **six** is just for you two
Please come up and stand next to me, **Lisa and Howie** this one's for you

Cousins Sara and Rachel; Samantha and Jenny, too
I love you all, and am thrilled to be, sharing this day with you
(Or if only two people, for first line use - Cousins Sara and Rachel, this candle is for you)

40

Sandy and Al, Allison and Bill, Marla and Fred, too
Robin and Mike, Barbara and Dave, Kim and Scott; please come up all
of you

I'd love you both to come up now; I'm so thrilled that you could be
Such an important part of my special day, it means so much to me

It's your turn now, so please come up and light this candle with me
**Erin, David, Michael, Austin and Jessi (use with any name ending with
the long E sound)**

I wish you guys lived closer to us; just think how great that would be
Roz, Chuck, Nicole, Danielle and Elyse come up here with me

Absent Guests

Use these sentiments when someone who would light a candle cannot attend. If any other members of his/her immediate family will be there, and lighting a candle, use one of these as an opening verse for that candle. If no one else from his or her family will be lighting a candle, you can use it as any numbered candle. Have your child light the candle himself.

I wish Aunt Jane could be here now; no words could possibly convey
She knows how much I love her; and our hearts are with her today
She would have lit this candle herself and danced with this wonderful crowd
So I'll light it for her and we'll all send love; I know she'll be very proud

Aunt Betty, I know you are proud today, though you're not here physically
I feel your love; I miss you so much. You mean the world to me

Even though they couldn't be here, I will take this time to say
Len and Geri and Norma Jean, I'm thinking of you today
Or
Grandpa Manny, I love you, I'm thinking of you today

Cousin David couldn't make it today, although he wanted to
He just couldn't avoid it; there was something he had to do

But I don't want this day to go by, without honoring him, too
So **Cousin David**, I love you; this one is for you

I'm sorry **Eddie** couldn't be here; I miss **Aaron, David and Judy** too
But I'm glad you're here to be with us; **Gloria**, this candle's for you

I grew up on stories of Gertie; they always made me laugh
Sylvia and Frank, it's an honor that you are here on her behalf

Family Friends

This group of folks are my parent's best friends. Their bond has held strong through the years
They are always there for each other; true friends through laughter and tears
I love hanging with you guys; we eat, and laugh and have fun
Squeeze in close as I call you; this will be a tight one
Dana, Gail, Michelle and Patty, Fred and Robert, too
Joe, Cory, Kirk and Elaine; please come up guys, I love you

Robin is one of my **Mom's** best friends; I'm delighted that you came
I know it's hard to come in from **New York**; but without you it's not the same

I love to go to your house; your bar-b-cues beat all the rest
We always have such a wonderful time; you guys are really the best

Alan and Sherry mean so much to us; you're my parent's best friends, you see
You've always been such a part of my life, you're more than just friends; you're family

When I want to know the latest styles, to find out what's modish and chic
To know what's classic or merely a fad; it's **Lorraine's** opinion I seek

This group of folks are my parent's best friends. Their bond has held strong through the years
They are always there for each other; true friends through laughter and tears

Melissa, Stan, Jennie and Jeff, Beth and Gary, too
I hope when I become an adult, I have friends that compare to you

This next group are family friends. Our get-togethers are really a hoot
You've been good friends for such a long time. And us kids are following suit

We've gone so many places with you; I couldn't name them all
But surely I remember, we always had a ball

What can I say about this crowd; they're my parent's closest friends
When we all get together, the laughter and fun never ends

Len, Geri, Ida, Maureen, Andy, Norman and Sheila, too
I've known you guys all my life; you know how I feel about you

One bam, two crack; the women like to say
They cackle and laugh a lot, as they sit around and play

I'd like you all to meet **Liz**; she's my **mother's** closest friend
Our two families travel together a lot; our good times never end

The **Goldberg** clan is fantastic: They're great friends who are special to me
Their house is really my second home; even their **dogs** are like my family

I look forward to our times together; our families have been friends for so long
I love to be around you guys; you treat me like I belong

There are some other folks here, who mean a lot to my family
They are good friends of my mom and dad and mean so much to me

Donna is my mom's best friend; when we're with you we have such a ball
We've gone so many places with you; I couldn't name them all

I love hanging out with you guys; we eat and laugh and have fun
Squeeze in close as I call you; this will be a tight one

*****

Sometimes you are just lucky when friends are like family
That's how we feel about you all, please come up and stand with me

We take such fun trips together; what great times, I know you agree
Beth and Gary, Lorraine and Jay, come on up and be here with me

You know how I feel about you and what you mean to my family
I love you, **Alyse and Lee,** I'm so glad you're here with me

So, **Michael** if you'll please come up and light a candle, too
It means so much to **Dad** and me that I could share this with you **(my parents)**

I've known you folks for so long. So, of course I'd want you to be
Honored on this special day, please come and stand with me

I want to thank you, **Elaine,** for helping Mom to plan for today
This candle is meant just for you; **Elaine** please come up right away

Jennifer, please come up now, and stand here next to me
You're more than just a family friend; you *are* my family

The families **Langsbard, Schwartz and Levine**; please come up and stand with me
You've always been such a part of my life. You're more than just friends; you're family

Bonnie, Marty, Zita, Jay, Beth and Gary, too
Lorraine and Jay, Lee and Alyse, please come up guys, I love you

We've known you guys forever. You're more than just friends; it's true
Allison, David, Jeff and Suzanne; come up guys; I love you

Judy, Mike, Stephanie and Sean; please come and stand with me
I love you guys, you're more than friends; you *are* my family

Child's Friends

To keep the ceremony as short as possible, use one candle for all your child's friends. Unless, the camp friends are really special to your child, one candle should be fine. Besides, it's always funny to see 40 or 50 of your child's "closest friends" come up together.

I'd like you all to meet my friends; these kids are really cool
Some are from the neighborhood; the others are from school
We have fun playing video games, riding our bikes or just hanging out
Going to the movies and Mario's, is what life's all about
We always have such great times, think of all the stuff we've been through
Come on up all my friends, I've saved this candle for you

I'd like you to meet my girlfriends; these kids are really cool
They're family friends, Hebrew buds and girls I know from school

All my friends are around me; from school and camp you're here
From Hebrew and the neighborhood, I've known you guys for years

I'd like you all to meet my friends; these kids are really cool
Some are from the neighborhood; the others are from school

We've known each other for so long; even though I've moved we're still tight
Eric, you're one of my oldest friends. I'm glad you're with me tonight

We have **fun playing video games, riding our bikes or just hanging out**
Going to the **movies** and **Mario's**, is what life's all about

I'd like to introduce this next group; these kids are friends of mine
We spend our time just hanging out, on the phone or chatting on line

We do everything together; it started when we were small
We skate, talk on line, we do our nails (use any activities) and we love to roam the mall

Now I'll bring up all my friends, each so special in their own unique way
Time won't allow for naming each one, but there's so much that I'd like to say

We have **fun playing video games**; our times together are never a bore
Just hanging out is great with you guys; hey, that's what good friends are for

In good times and bad times your friendships shine through
You can always count on me to be there for you

*****

We always have such great times, think of all the stuff we've been through
Come on up all my friends, I've saved this candle for you

I know you all for quite a while; the greatest friends there ever could be
You know I think you're all the best. Candle **twelve** is yours, come stand with me

You know I think you're all special, but it's worth saying again
Squeeze in tight, all my friends so you can all light candle ten

All my friends are so special; they're from home, school and family
Come on up now, this one's for you; you all mean so much to me

We always have such excellent times. Friends like you are seldom and few
Please come up all my friends, I've saved this candle for you

I thank you all for being here; as far as friends go, you are great!
Please come up here all my friends; hurry, don't make me wait

Camp friends

We look forward to being together, at **Camp Ben-Ann** where summers are great
If only the boys would finally grow; I can't imagine how long we must wait

You are my summer sisters; I love you all and you'll agree
Our **senior** summer will really rock. Come up now and stand with me

We look forward to being together and for winter to end, we can't wait
We love **Color War, the socials, the sports,** at **Camp Belmont** where summers are great

So be with me now, all my camp friends; I'm so happy you're all here today
I've saved this candle just for you, so please come up right away

For years we've all lived together. **Camp Timberlake's** great, you'll agree
We've been together for such a long time; you **guys** mean so much to me
(all)

And this summer will be no different. We'll rock the camp; we're so cool
You know we'll have the most awesome time, cause everyone knows **seniors** rule!

Throughout the cold, long winter, our memory of camp never fades
The sports, color war, the socials and trips; the Olympics, the **girls**, Ahhhh the raids
(boys)

We're going to be **seniors** this year; the camp is in for quite a shock
Candle nine is for my **Camp Pocono** friends; you know I think you guys rock!

Best Friends

I love hanging out and talking to boys, with these friends of mine
And when we have nothing to do, we'll do our hair a hundred times

Though all my friends are super, these **three** are special to me
So please come up **Sara, Jen and Dana;** I really love you three

You are my best friend, **Brittany.** We have such a great time together
I know we'll always feel this way; cause we'll be best friends forever

We love hanging out together; at the mall we love spending our day
You'll always find us on the phone or on line just chatting away

Though all my friends are super, these girls are special to me
So please come up **Ashley, Angela, Nicole, Courtney, Melissa and Mallory (end with a name that ends in the long E sound)**

We tell each other everything; we gossip on the phone and on line
Emily, Rachel and Rebecca; please come light candle nine

Though all my friends are special, this guy just stands out from the rest
We do everything together; **Corey**, you are the best

This next guy is my very best friend; I've known him for so long
We're always together, where ever we go; our friendship will always stay strong

We've been through so much already; our friendship is tried and true
Matt, my pal, come on up; this one is just for you.

Siblings

Siblings can each have their own candles. If you already have too many candles, bring them up together; just include them all in the poem. Have them stay up (off to the side) after their turn. Parents are next and the photographer likes a picture with the whole family blowing out the candles.

My sister Rachel can always be found, on the cell phone with a friend
She'll shop till she drops; and we all who know, how much money she can spend
The boys love to talk to her; cause she's pretty and so cool
You're always watching out for me, as sisters go, you rule
She's active in sports and loves AOL; IM her, you know that she'll answer
Turn on the music and watch her go, she is such a wonderful dancer
I wouldn't trade you for anyone else; a sister couldn't ask for more
Rachel, I love you, come stand with me, you're the sister that I adore

My brother is so handsome and bright; he's the smartest person I know
He always watches out for me; I'm so proud that he is my 'bro"

Stacy, it's true I borrow your clothes. Why do yours seem better than mine?
It's true we fight, but all sisters do. I love you *most* of the time

Then there's my **little sister**, **Danielle;** as good and sweet as can be
She's spoiled rotten, but that's OK, cause she is so special to me

Sam just got his license, and the folks just bought him a car
Frankly, I'm thrilled; it keeps him away. I love him when he is afar

Sandy, you know, I love you. We have fun most of the time
We're great at annoying our parents; after all, we're partners in crime

My sister is always so trendy; with her clothing, hair products, cologne
She loves to dance, will shop till she drops. She can always be found on the phone

I really love my **kid brother (big sister),** although **he** can be quite a pain
Sometimes **he** is so annoying, I think I might go insane

Adam now has his license. Let's go out and give it a whirl
And while we're at it, **brother,** I need your advice about a girl

We've always been so very close; on you I can depend
You're more than just my **sister**; you are my special friend

We do always fight; don't we **Sarah?** But I'm not unhappy, I'm glad
After all, what would we do with our time? And it sure does make Mom and
Dad mad

I love when your friends come over; they're so hot; they can make a guy
drool
I'm glad you're my older sister; **Marissa,** you're really cool

My sister **Lauren** can always be found on the cell phone with a friend
She'll shop till she drops and we all know, how much money she can spend

She's active in sports and loves AOL; IM her you know that she'll answer
Turn on the music and watch her go; she is such a wonderful dancer

I know that we fight all the time; but that's what **brothers** are for
We're the best of friends at the end of the day; **Jordan,** no one could love
you more

And here's my **sister Jenny**; she loves to shop and talk on the phone
Sometimes she drives me crazy and our fights can sure be full-blown

I love my little brother **Josh**; we spend as much time together as we can
You think everything I do is so cool; you are my biggest fan

We've been going to camp together, these summers are favorites of mine
You know, we're making enough memories to last a whole lifetime

When I need help on the computer, there's one person I always ask
My **older sister Jennifer**; she's always up to the task

Justin and Jacob, my **brothers**; you know how much I love you
Sometimes you drive me crazy; but I guess that's what **little brothers** do

I will always watch out for you guys, you can always expect me to be
Right by your sides, or anytime, **either** of you guys need me **(any)**

Rachel goes to college now; I miss you, I really do
Cause you're not around to fight with; I bet you miss it, too

You always give me fashion advice. Your fun jokes just make me scream
Most times, you are really nice; when you're not being a "Drama Queen"

*****

I'm only kidding siblings; I know you'll both agree
We'll always be there for each other; come up now and be with me

I wouldn't trade you for anyone else, a **sister** couldn't ask for more
Justin and Jacob come on up now, you're the **brothers** that I adore

I wouldn't trade her for anyone else; a **brother** couldn't ask for more
Jessi, come up light this one, you're the **sister** that I adore

My brother and I are spirited; we'll compete till the bitter end
But it's all in fun, I love you **Josh;** you're my brother and my best friend

I'm delighted you're my **sister**; our friendship and love will not end
I'm a lucky **older brother**; **Jaclyn,** my sister, my friend

You know I'm only kidding, and how much I love you; it's true
Please come up now my **sister Marissa**; this candle is just for you

As a **brother** you're loving and caring; you know I depend upon you
We'll always have each other; **Austin,** this one's for you

I love when you hang out with me; I look forward to the times that you do
As brothers go, you are the 'bomb"; Come up **Grant,** I love you

I'm so glad you're my younger **sister;** our friendship and love will not end
I know we'll be best pals for life; **Rachel,** my **sister,** my friend

As far as **older brothers** go; you're really cool; it's true
Scott, please come up now; you know Bro, I love you

Sometimes you drive me crazy; I guess that's what **little brothers** do
But you are cool most of the time; **Ben**, you know I love you

I want you both to realize, I will always be there for you
So come up now **Jason** and **Casey**, this candle is just for you two

Jennifer is a great role model; she's smart and good; it's true
I always have you to look up to; I love you **Jen**, this one's for you

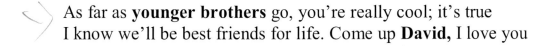As far as **younger brothers** go, you're really cool; it's true
I know we'll be best friends for life. Come up **David,** I love you

Parents

Here is a sample of a Parents' candle. It's just a sample; feel free to make it your own by adding personal activities, nick names, etc. Everyone listens to this one…make it count.

This one is for my Mom and Dad, I'm sure that you'll agree
They are a wonderful couple; they do so much for me
Mom helps me with my homework; she's always busy running around
Taking care of all our needs in a house where love abounds
Dad always wants the best for me. He's such fun; just like a friend
He coaches my teams, plays ball with me; our good times just don't end
I love how you two respect me; you really listen to what I say
I feel your love, your strength, your pride, surround me every day
I thank you both for everything and for giving me this day to shine
Now together let's blow out these candles, and let's all have a wonderful time

Mom is always yelling at me; "Stop watching TV all of the time"
My room is always a dirty mess. Tell me; is that really such a crime?

Dad, I'm always asking, "Take me there? Can you buy me some?
And no, I don't have a job and I know where the money comes from

If a contest for best mom was held, I know that mine would win
Except maybe for the cooking part. What's for dinner Mom; should we call in?

My Mom, you gotta love her; she can't cook to save her life
But that's OK; cause other than that, she's the most awesome mother and wife

Dad, I love when we hang out; we have fun whatever we do
We **golf and play ball**. You know what, Dad? I hope I grow up just like you. **(any activity)**

My Dad really loves to cook; his recipes are great
We love to go to movies, or just hang out and stay up late

Mom, you're such a role model; you're as loving and smart as can be
But don't sing in the car, with my friends; you know it embarrasses me

Dad, you embarrass me in front of my friends. Your singing simply must stop
You should see the clothes I hide from you, after **Grandma** and I shop

My Dad lives and breathes the market; when it's up we all say, "Amen"
You know why we all feel that way? Cause Mom's gone out shopping again

Mom, you've taught me to be self-sufficient; I can cook and wash my clothes, too
I know how to clean up after myself. One day, some girl will thank you

You guys drive me all over; you are constantly running it seems
It's **basketball or la cross** or one of my other sports teams

My Mom, she does love shopping and our closets she sure does fill
I love all the stuff, and try not to laugh, while she passes Dad the bill

Some kids are embarrassed by their folks, but my Mom and Dad are real cool
Mom buys me pretty much everything; Dad can fix anything with a tool

I know that I procrastinate; I leave everything till the last minute
But if I became timely and prompt, it wouldn't be me; would it?

My Mom's not too swift with a needle and thread. Scissors and glue really put her to the test
But put a credit card in her hand, step back, watch what she does best

I love how you two respect me; you really listen to what I say
I feel your love, your strength, your pride, surround me every day

This one is for my Mom and Dad; I'm sure that you'll agree
They are a wonderful couple; they do so much for me

You help me with my homework; all you do shows me you care
I appreciate that you *try* to cook; I try not to tease you when you err

Mom is involved in all I do. She says' "There aren't enough hours in the day"
She's always running, taking care of our needs. No time to cook. We'll eat out? OK

My Dad can fix anything. He teaches me everything, too
He always gives me all he's got and helps me with all that I do

We have great times in our house; we're quite a boisterous crowd
You can hardly hear what's being said 'cause we're all so very loud

Mom always repeats herself when she gives me something to do
She says it over and over again; **Mom**, do you think I can't hear you?

Dad is always bugging me to go to my room and clean
Come on **Dad,** what was your room like, when you were just thirteen?

Mom, you're the best class mother; there is no task that's ever too much
You're amazing at whatever you do; we always count on your special touch

Dad, you've always been there for me. You've coached all of my sports teams
You take the time to show you care and I know how much that means

You know I'm "Daddy's Little Girl"; he'll do anything for me
That's just where Daddy's like to be--wrapped around their daughter's pinky

*****

You know I'm only kidding, you support me in all that I do
Thank you for this wonderful day, Mom and Dad, I love you

I want you to know I realize, and appreciate all that you do
I'll take this time to thank you both; Mom and Dad, I love you

Mom and Dad are always right by my side; they support me in all that I do
Thank you for this wonderful day. Mom and Dad, I love you

I thank you both for everything and for giving me this day to shine
Now together let's blow out these candles, and let's all have a wonderful time

Mother/ Father Alone/ with other significant other – you can also use these, if appropriate, for any parents' candle.

Mom, we just have each other; we really make quite a team
You surround me with your love each day; I know you share my dreams
I feel blessed that we have each other; no words could ever say
I love you Mom; together we're strong. I thank God for you each day.

I know how much you love me; you show me in every way
Come on up **Dad,** I love you; today and every day

Dad, you always make the effort; it's not easy, but you do
You are so important in my life; come up **Dad**, I love you

To bring all parents up together:
This candle is for my parents. I know that you'll agree
They are **two wonderful couples**; they mean so much to me
        (four wonderful people, 3 wonderful people, etc.)

I love the time I spend with you I look forward to the weekend
We really have a great time, **Dad**, my buddy, my friend

You make me do my homework, but you help me so that's cool
Dad, you know I love you, you're the bomb; you know you rule!

This candle is just for you; **Mom**, thank you for all you do
I feel your strength, your pride, your love; you know how I love you

When I spend my time with you guys; the feelings are very strong
I always have a really good time; you make me feel as if I belong

Now here's my **Dad and Lacy**; we're together on the weekend
I love our times together, **Lacy**, I feel like you're my friend

Dad and Lacy please come up; I know that you'll agree
We love each other. Thanks for today. Come take your place with me

Mom you always support me; your encouragement sees me through
I thank you for always being there; **Mom**, you know I love you

I can talk to my **mom** about anything; her advice is always grade A
We'll always be there for each other; **Mom**, thanks for this wonderful day

Mom, I know it's not easy; you work and take care of me
I know I should be easier; I'm sure that you agree

I really appreciate how you take care of **us**; on your own, I know it's rough
You work so hard to keep **us** happy; for you, nothing is ever too tough

Everything **Mom** does for **us**, has her remarkable touch
Thank you **Mom** for all you do, I love you very much

Mom and David thank you, for everything you do
I love you both very much; this most special candle is for you

Parent to Child

This is a nice little touch to end the candle lighting ceremony. You can use this time to tease your child a little bit. Mention that she is a slob, always forgets her books in school, talks too much on the phone, etc. Always include her good attributes, as well. Mom should say a verse or two. Then Dad can wind it up with a verse to your child and an invitation for everyone to "party." If you are having a "good luck" candle do not use this, too; this should be your last poem.

Mom says:
What can we say about you, Sami; we're so proud of all that you do
You are so sweet, so loving, so kind. God has surely blessed us with you
You're such an energetic kid; you love to dance and sing and shop
You play your sports, you hang with your friends; your activities never stop
Dad says:
As always, Sami you light up our lives, and today is your day to shine
Now you light this last birthday candle; and let's all have a wonderful time

Of course it's tough to wake you; it's hard to get your day to start
Yet you talk so fast, it's hard to keep up; but it's OK, cause most of it's smart

What can we say about you, **Jenny;** we're so proud of all that you do
You are so sweet, so loving, so kind. No child could bring more joy than you

I have so much to say about you, Jordan. Dad and I are so proud of all you do
You're a loyal, true friend, with talent and wits; God has surely blessed us with you

What can we say about you, **Zach?** We're so proud of all that you do
You're funny, smart, sensitive, kind. We are surely, blessed with you

We love that you and your **sister**, are so close it makes us glad
I know I've said it, but I'll say it again, you're the two best kids a **Mom** ever had

Danielle, we love watching you grow; like a flower we've seen you bloom
You want to grow up, seek wisdom and truth; but first will you clean up your room?

David your TV is always so loud, it really makes my ears ring
It makes me nuts, but I've found out, you can't help it; it's a "guy" thing

You put us through our paces; you know just what I mean
It took all our will, our love, our strength, to let you live to see thirteen

I love the times when we just chill; we hang out together each day
You confide in me, we laugh a lot; **Josh**, I love you in every way

Scott, you're an **awesome drummer**; your talents really shine through
If only you practiced a little bit, imagine how well you would do

Jon, your life runs in slow motion; always late, always overdue
Except when your friends call, boy do you run; faster than we can say, "Boo"

As always, we love and respect you. Today is your day to shine
Now you light this last candle and let's all have a wonderful time

As always, **Jaclyn,** you light up our lives, and today is your day to shine
Now you light this last birthday candle; and let's all have a wonderful time

You know we're only teasing; we love you with all of our might
Now you light this last candle, and we'll get on with this wonderful night

You worked so hard to prepare for today. You were awesome, we all agree
So light this last one, we'll get on with the fun; now let's all go and "party"

We wish you pride and strength, my son. You'll always be our little boy
If God grants you a fraction of what we wish, you'll be blessed with a life full of joy

Good Luck

Not everyone uses a good luck candle in his/her ceremony. If you do choose to have one, it is the last candle. Your child will light this one and use it to thank everyone for coming. It's customary for the whole family to blow out the candles together. If you opt for a welcome candle, you don't really need a good luck candle. If you choose a parent to child candle, do not use this good luck candle.

Some families place one tall candle on each table and invite everyone to stand and light it together. I've written a closing line for it (last verse in chapter). It's a nice finish. Don't forget to put matches on the adult tables if you do this.

With the richness of tradition and all it represents,
I hope I have conveyed to you with these sentiments
How fortunate I feel to have a family such as this
If I didn't take this moment now, I know I'd feel remiss
So I'll light this last candle, with my family surrounding me
Let's wish for peace around the world and may every one live free

Well this is it; I made it. I never imagined it would be
As wonderful as it is right now; I'm so pleased you're all with me

Thank you for coming from near and far; to celebrate my **Bat Mitzvah** day
It makes me feel so special, to be surrounded by you today

I know that I'm a lucky kid to have such great friends and family
I'll light this good luck candle now, wishing *you* peace and harmony

Thank you all for coming to celebrate my **Bar** Mitzvah day
I know some of you traveled from a far distance away

My family wants to thank you and I will thank you, too
My day was made so special, and it's all because of you

If I called up everyone I loved, you'd all be standing here
We wouldn't have time for anything else; you're all so very dear

I'm a lucky **guy** to be loved this much; and now I'll end this rhyme
I'll blow out all the candles, and let's all have a wonderful time

How lucky I feel to have friends and family such as you
Always there to be supportive, kind and loving, too

I know that I'm a lucky guy, and not every kid lives this way
So, I've donated some of my **Bar Mitzvah** gifts, in honor of today

There is a candle on each table, please stand and light it with me
Let's wish for peace around the world and may everyone live free